Introduction

When Shawn my husband was diagnosed wit
as I knew it was about to change. He had bec
life, my happy ever after so how could it be all coming to an end. Why was he leaving, why was this happening?

This book is a collection of poems I wrote as I faced going down the path of losing my husband to cancer, whilst discovering a new journey that was all about the true gift of love and how opening up to self-love could one day lead to finding me...

"It's all about the love," Shawn said to me as we chatted on what I didn't know at the time was his final day here with me. It's only now I am fully starting to understand what that meant.

Love is who we are and it is the most powerful energy we have. It all starts from within and when you start to learn this, you are then open to all it brings which is joy, freedom and inner peace.

It is with love that I wanted to share my poems, and this book is a dedication to my darling Shawn of the journey we started together and I now continue alone. It's my wish that the poems on the following pages help you see the light even on your darkest of days and that you come to the realization that life really is all about love, it never leaves it merely transcends.

From my heart to yours

Kerry x

Sunshine Moments

During Shawn's 18-month battle with cancer, I was constantly trying to find positives in each day to try and shift the focus from all the negativity. The analogy of seeking my sunshine moments was born and very quickly became a massive part of helping me cope then and still does now.

We can't control what happens to us but we can choose how we respond to it and I am a firm believer that the pendulum of life swings both ways. Change is a certainty, as is the weather but a consistence is the sun, it always shines even behind the clouds. So with this in mind I face each day letting the clouds come and go as the winds of change pass through, knowing I can always look for a ray of sunshine somewhere somehow…

Yes, some days are harder than others, as the sky can appear full of clouds sometimes; big black ones full of rain but I know in my heart I choose to look for the rays of light from the sun to brighten my darkest days.

I wrote the following poem to describe what sunshine moments are; I truly hope you take inspiration from this book and start to seek and indeed find lots in your days too.

Sunshine Moments

Sunshine moments are what we look for in our everyday,
Especially when the clouds come along before they drift away.

The clouds are the challenges we come across in life,
You know the ones that give us grief and plenty of strife.

So when the clouds come in order to help them fade,
We look for sunshine moments to brighten up our day.

The clouds will keep on coming every day you'll see,
They're part of our life's teachings, yes for you and for me.

So when they come along as hard as it may be,
Allow them to float on past and in time you will see.

Switching your focus is what you need to do,
Finding the sunshine to stop you from feeling blue.

It's magical when this happens you open up your heart,
Life starts flowing again and you look forward not to the past.

Your energy changes for all around to see,
You start working from the We instead of the Me.

Your rays of light shine so brightly all around,
A new way of looking at life you have surely found.

It's time now to spread your wings and go forward in your light,
To all who witness you, it becomes a beautiful sight.

Cancer it's not the end

Cancer comes into your life and throws your world upside down,
As it shakes you up and spins you around.

So many emotions you never knew existed,
Some of them feel quite bitter and twisted.

Thoughts in your head, start to run riot,
And you long for the moments of peace & the quiet.

Forever racing they never leave you alone,
Fear and anxiety become a familiar tone.

Your life has changed from a world you once knew,
New eyes are now what you clearly look through.

Time takes on new meaning as it pulls at your heart,
Fearing for loved ones never wanting to part.

Quality not quantity is what matters now,
You focus on being, not wondering how.

Grabbing each day knowing you're alive,
After all, we came here to grow and thrive.

And if it's your journey that the end time is here,
Then you'll know in your heart, it's perfectly clear.

You're going home to that place you once knew,
Where others await you as their time, it came too.

We are here on this earth for such a short time it's true,
Each of us is born with a mission to do.

To love and be loved is what most of us seek,
A power we know to be strong, not weak.

Love is what goes on when it comes to the end,
It does not leave it merely transcends.

So yes we fear leaving our physical body parts,
But the soul remains solid, living on in other's hearts

Dear Cancer,

I want you to know as you manipulate your way through people's lives, our life trying to destroy everything in your path.
You've taken and continue to try to take what you can, yet I've gained so much.

I've never known so much sorrow yet felt so much joy.
You've stolen relationships yet I've gained so many friends.
You've taken away my thoughts of the future yet I bask in the gift of time and memories.

You've shown me weakness yet taught me strengths I never knew I had.
You've shown me fear and yet again I have gained courage.
You see cancer there is no greater value than Love!

So whilst you twist and slither through our life causing destruction in your path and stripping us back to our bare souls, I know you cannot take or destroy love.
Love is the one thing even as you pick away at the physical body that cannot be taken.

It's who we are, it's the one common denominator we all have and can control.
In a world where we can lose sight and focus on all we don't have or can't do, Love is always the one thing we can have, be and do!
It's free to give and priceless to receive, no matter what you take, love is always there to hold onto.

So cancer yes there are days when the fight gets me down, after all, that's what fighting does it takes your energy, whereas love will lift it and that's what I choose.
Self-love has shown me when people say, "Be strong" that I have a new understanding of what that means. Being strong is who I am, it's not just showing up with a smile and a positive attitude, it's saying this f**king sucks and today I'm not feeling strong, today I feel weak, today I want to hide away and not talk, not smile, not put on a brave face. Today I want to show I'm scared and feel sad about my future that has now all changed.

Life has no control button on it and we just have to ride it. Being strong is having the courage to scream, shout and cry if you want to, it's all just shit! Allowing others to share in your vulnerability and say it's ok to not be ok, that's being strong and yes cancer you've taught me that!

So whilst some say you go through an anger stage and yes that may still come, I don't feel anger or hate at this moment. I only feel love because; that my friend is and always will be completely indestructible and something that you can't touch.

With Love

Kerry Knight

It's time...

The time has come and you're moving on,
Please wait one more minute that's all I want.

If only time stood still a button I could press,
It could take away this aching in my chest.

Life doesn't work that way we sadly know,
It's time to leave so my sorrow grows.

Your last physical breath I watched you take,
Inside my heart, I can feel it break.

I love you; I'm not ready for you to leave,
My mind is racing, begging; don't take him, please.

The angels are here though to guide you safely,
To the other side where loved ones do wait.

Ones like you who have gone before,
They are there greeting you at the open door.

Emigrated to heaven is what I choose to believe,
You've gone home early where you'll be waiting for me.

It's not my time yet I have much still to do,
This you know and believe to be true.

So up in heaven, you will sit and wait,
Until it's my time then you'll be at the gate.

I know you'll be there waiting for me,
With that big beaming smile full of glee.

For now, I must carry on living this life,
Being every day thankful I am your wife.

Sleep tight my darling each night I will say,
As I look at the stars with a tearful gaze.

The night sky it's gained one shining so bright,
Our love I will hold and treasure so tight.

Nothing lasts forever people often say,
But we found a love that's here to stay.

Where do we go?

When we die where do we go?
It's something for us still living, we never know.

Do we join the stars in the big night sky?
Or is there really, a heaven that floats on high?

Some people believe in heaven and hell
Only you don't get to choose so that doesn't sit well.

Is there a God and devil out there?
Some say yes and you better beware.

For me, I like to believe we leave this place,
For it then creates another person's space.

Our soul goes back home to where they came from,
Yet still, we remain in the hearts of those who long.

The ones left behind find it hardest to bare,
They just can't believe we are no longer there.

The sadness the heartache of not physically seeing,
That person they so loved as a human being.

In time, it is said this feeling will pass,
We have memories that were built and made to last.

I've gone back home please don't be sad,
I promise you life will not be that bad.

You see one day you get to join the special club with me,
And together again are hearts united will be.

This club has a special entry date,
But that you don't know it's down to fate.

I'll be there waiting with a big beaming smile,
Then you will know I've been with you all the while.

Only in death do we get to see,
That we all actually, live in eternity.

The wind, the trees the bird flying high,
They are all signs I'm with you, nearby.

As souls, we live in everything all around,
Not in one body can we be found.

So the next time you feel the wind touch your face,
Know it is me entering your space.

I'll always be with you in your living years,
So please don't be sad and dry your tears.

Live life happy, full and free,
For one day you know you'll be back with me.

When you truly love someone they are never gone,
Love is eternal it lives on and on.

How do I feel?

People, keep asking me how I feel?
The truth is I don't know it doesn't seem real.

I can't comprehend the thoughts in my head,
as I still think I'll find you sleeping in my bed.

It's like a dream I'll soon be awake,
this all feels like such a terrible mistake.

You'll walk through the door after a hard day's work,
with that big cheeky grin giving me a smirk.

We will sit over a cuppa chatting about our day,
discussing whom we've met along the way.

The kids will soon come bounding in,
I'll raise an eyebrow at them for interrupting.

I've got lots to tell you that's important you see,
Only they don't realise you're sitting with me.

They can't see you in that empty chair,
to them, it seems there's nobody there.

But I see you everywhere that I look;
It's like opening up a memory book.

From the moment I wake, I think of you,
so you not being here just can't be true.

Sadly I know I must accept our fate,
so for another time with you, I'll have to wait.

My dreams are where we meet up now,
I don't question it or wonder how.

It's the only way we get to be,
together again just you and me.

I called out your name the other day;
Silence was all that came my way.

In time I guess I'll learn you've gone,
But in my heart always you'll live on and on.

I miss you

The nights are the hardest I find to bear,
When all I can do is lay here and stare.

The emptiness of what was once your space,
How I long to see and touch your face.

No longer does your body lay next to mine,
Our hearts no longer beat in perfect time.

It's these times I greet my familiar friend,
His name is loneliness and it starts to descend.

The darkness starts to gather around,
I call out to you but you're nowhere to be found.

It's at times like this I feel so alone,
Wanting to hear your voice, that familiar tone.

You said you'd never leave me,
Sadly it wasn't meant to be.

I know it wasn't your choice you had to go,
If it had been, you'd clearly have said no.

I must face life living without you now,
Some days I stand and wonder exactly how?

But go on I will without you here,
Even though at times I'm filled with fear.

For you my love I promise to stay strong,
I'll keep your memory going on.

I'll stand tall and proud as your wife,
Continue to live a happy life.

Through the children, I'll always see,
The love we have you and me.

In the darkness of the night,
I'll look to my heart for the light.

You are always there in that special place,
My memories will show me your smiling face.

I'll drift off to sleep the tears will subside,
In my dreams I know you'll be by my side.

Miss you babe's xx

The Butterfly that flew away

One day a butterfly came my way,
It landed on me and chose to stay.

Out of all the places, it could land,
It chose me and took my hand.

Its beauty was a marvel for all to see,
I'm so thankful out of all the choices it chose me.

This butterfly stayed for quite a while,
I often looked with love and a smile

Then the day came it had to fly away,
No longer with me could it stay.

Its tragic and sad people would say,
I choose to look at it another way.

I focus on the love, and not the loss,
The here and now, not the was.

That butterfly was my husband you see,
Of all the people of this world, he chose me.

So that love is what's here to stay,
I'm not looking at a butterfly that flew away.

I see him often all around,
In my home and children, he is found.

So that butterfly came with a message to say,
There is always love it never fly's away.

The Uninvited Friend

Have you met my new friend his name is Grief?
Popping in often, sometimes keeping it brief.

Other times he likes a longer time, to stay,
without a care, he's getting in your way.

Your life he seems to think he controls,
I've got news for him and he needs to be told.

You weren't invited to be my friend,
but I'll see it through to the bitter end.

I'll show you we can live side by side,
Even though at times you make me cry.

It's not that I don't want you around;
I just don't want a permanent frown.

I accept you're here no leaving date,
your invite in; was all down to fate.

Some see you with fear and dread
knowing the tears you cause us to shed.

I choose to say we will become good friends,
I know your rules, which I will start to bend.

I won't let you rule my time each day,
You'll soon get to see, that I do it my way.

You're here as part of a natural force,
Straight to the heart my route to, source.

The heart is where the healing must start,
it's broken and shattered it fell apart.

Slowly though we will rebuild it to be whole,
as I know deep down this is your role.

Grief, I know you're here for a reason,
A lifetime I guess not just a season.

So uninvited you were at first,
without you though my tears wouldn't burst.

I choose to see the good in all that you do;
in my heart, I know it to be true.

Time is your friend you bring along,
it's your gift to me and I hear his song.

Time does not heal all wounds they say;
yet to heal we need time to sit and pray.

You're here to help me get life back again,
my dear and special uninvited friend.

To grieve is a sign to the ones we love,
watching down on us from heaven above.

We miss you and longingly wish you were here,
But grief is the friend now who holds you near.

So come on in don't be shy,
it's ok if I start to cry.

It's only grief my newfound friend,
He becomes everyone's friend, in the end.

Life's a pendulum!

Some days you're up, some days you're down
Some days you smile whilst others you frown.

After a high, there seems a low,
It's the pendulum of life and how it flows.

One day you're happy full of glee,
The next you're weeping, saying how can this be?

Life's a rollercoaster twisting up and down,
You feel shaken up and thrown around.

Holding on is all you can do,
Even more tightly when you're feeling blue.

Trust the pendulum is what I will say,
The fact remains it swings both ways.

So ride the waves of sadness with time,
It's a long way up this mountain to climb.

When you get to the top you will see,
Everything has worked out as it's meant to be.

The clouds, part and start to clear,
And once again the sunshine appears.

Yep trust this pendulum of life I say,
Things will become good again one day.

Nothing stays the same for you and me,
It's the changes of life I hereby decree.

Just go with the swinging of its chimes,
Knowing the bad always changes back to good times.

The pendulum of life can swing slow or fast,
Its job is to keep you moving forward, not in the past.

It's the pendulum of life swinging both ways,
Remember this on your cloudy days.

When four became three!

There's an aching in my heart,
It's breaking being torn apart.

Our beautiful little family,
Went from being four to now just three.

I can't stop my tears from starting to flow,
As I sit here watching our children grow.

Their little hearts are aching too,
For the love they have and miss from you.

I can do nothing to ease their pain,
Except to trust and have faith in the strength they will gain.

Their young delicate lives, thrown up in the air,
It feels like all I can do is watch in despair.

Why did life give us this terrible fate?
When death came to take you to the heaven gates.

A big empty hole in our home is felt now,
You're no longer there to kiss our brows.

An empty space on the sofa where you sat,
Reminds me of a time when we would laugh and chat.

Your voice, your laugh, we can no longer hear,
It's only found in memory, where we hold you, dear.

The photos we have to look at all around,
Bring thankfully more smiles than a sorrowful frown.

Yes, the family went from four to three,
In our hearts is where you'll always be.

We love you, we miss you more than words can say,
We think of you and talk of you every day.

Through us, you will continue to live on,
We don't really see you as truly gone.

In spirit and in all the energies around,
Is where we know you can now be found.

So as we whisper your name to say goodnight,
We catch a glimpse of your star it's shining bright.

A reminder to us you're always here,
In the darkness, we know you are always near.

Yes, our family has gone from four to three,
But I know deep down you're always next to me.

The Burnt Pizza!

I burnt the pizza tonight it made me cry,
The kids looked at me wondering why?

It wasn't the pizza that brought the tears,
It was the realisations of all my fears.

This life I'm now living all alone,
The reality hits your not coming home.

I'm learning to live this everyday life,
No longer are we, husband and wife.

I've got a new name now, a widow is what they say,
I didn't ask for it to be this way.

Sometimes I kickback and resent this newfound life,
The pain I feel cuts like a knife.

Others days I explore the adventures laying ahead,
It's like watching a movie whirl around my head.

Somehow I find the strength to get up each day,
Then on others under the duvet is where I want to stay.

Yes, the pizza burning caused me to cry,
You're not here is the real reason why.

Sleeping with the light on.

Sometimes the night seems so long,
I often sleep with the light switched on.

The darkness is so hard to bear,
Constantly knowing you're not there.

The coldness of the empty space,
No longer can I see your face.

I yearn to feel the warmth of your arms,
Holding me tight and safe from harm.

Your heartbeat I can no longer hear,
My eyes start to leak as I shed a tear.

I hate this feeling of being alone,
I want you here back at home.

I won't wake anymore to see you smile,
As you tell me it's ok to stay in bed for a while.

No longer is the school run a turn you take,
And tea in bed I now have to make.

It's all the little things I miss you see,
They were the pieces that made up you and me.

Like a jigsaw, we just fitted together,
Neither of us could have asked for better.

That jigsaw is broken and now fallen apart,
There's a piece missing from my heart.

The love we had felt so strong,
How did it all go so terribly wrong?

It's hurting again this deep pain I feel,
The life I now live is so different and surreal.

In time I'll learn to face the darkness into which I stare,
Knowing it's ok you'll always be there.

The passing of time is what's needed to heal,
This aching heart and sadness I feel.

From the darkness will eventually come the night,
I no longer feel the need, to leave on the light.

The Reading glasses

I tried to clear some of your clothes today,
Fold and arrange them to put away.

Some into bags off to charity to be sold,
Some I have to keep, a little longer for me to hold.

I stumbled on your reading glasses waiting to be found,
The grief hit me, I was floored and on the ground.

The pain in my heart was so hard to bare,
I wanted to reach out to you, but you're not there.

Memories flashed by me with each shirt I did fold,
As a reminder of all the stories one day to be told.

I stopped to sniff searching for that familiar smell,
All trace of you gone, my eyes began to well.

I let the pain out from the deepest depth of my soul,
Knowing it's all part of the journey, to make me whole.

I must fully go into this grief, the sadness I feel,
It's a natural part of helping me heal.

I sat for a moment in a heap on the floor,
Desperately wishing you to walk through the door.

The silence soothed me and the feeling did pass,
The pain eased, I knew it wouldn't last.

I had a moment of courage knowing it was a step to take,
Maybe it was too soon a bit of a mistake.

I tried to clear some of your clothes today,
I'm not fully ready; I think I will leave for another day.

I think of you...

I think of you every single day,
you are on my mind in some little way.

A flash of memory stirs a smile,
others make me feel sad, for a while.

Sometimes a thought pops in my head,
of something to tell you that someone said.

Then I remember you're not here,
I can no longer tell you my hopes & fears.

Some days it's hard the emotions weigh me down,
I don't mean to carry this solemnly frown.

I miss your strong arms holding me tight.
The gentle kiss as you say Goodnight.

The way you looked at me with your cheeky grin,
it stole my heart and you'd always win.

I often tell stories of the things you'd do and say,
all the funny little things you did your way.

They make me laugh and make me cry,
my heart feels heavy and lets out a sigh.

I often think of you the memories so precious and dear,
Now that I don't have you, to hold and be near.

Thanks for popping in my head to visit every day,
I just wish you could stay and not go back away.

The Visit

At night when it's quiet all around,
In the darkness so still you can't hear a sound.

That's the time I know is free,
When you can visit, come and see me.

We smile and hug so thankfully,
Our moment in time just you and me.

Nobody else ever knows you are here,
And when you leave I shed a tear.

I'm thankful for us dancing freely under the stars,
No longer restrained by the grief with bars.

You are with me our souls once again re-unite,
As we chatter and laugh long into the night.

Then the time comes and you have to go,
It's part of the deal, this I always know.

It's the end of the night I'm starting to wake,
No longer am I in a dream-like state.

I'll have to wait until tonight when we once again meet,
In my dreams whilst I'm lying here fast asleep...

Grief...

Grievers don't need fixing they long to be heard,
they need your ears, not your well-intentioned words.

They need to release, their tears to flow free,
this can be challenging for you to see.

The natural impulse is to comfort and want to help,
as you're reminded of emotions you have also once felt.

You may even be tempted to offer these words,
"Be strong", "I know how you feel" and soon the griever is back to not being heard.

You may feel awkward offering no words instead,
the griever is left alone feeling isolated and filled with dread.

Will there ever be a time they don't feel so alone,
a familiar place they can once again call home?

The world they knew has changed, and fallen apart,
as they struggle to heal their broken heart.

Another false myth is time is a healer;
this is untrue and painful to the griever.

Instead of offering words of advice,
simply sit with them in silence that would be nice.

Let them talk, tell all their hopes and fears,
be there as a big heart with open ears.

And if listening to them means your tears also flow,
Let that be ok here's what you should know.

Grieving is a natural emotion to change and loss,
not letting it happen can come at a cost.

Squashed down emotions over the years,
simply lead to more heartache and many more tears.

In order, to move forward, you need to let it all go;
Emotions are all part of the natural healing flow.

Lonely Evenings!

Most of the time I think I'm doing fine,
Then I sit down alone drinking wine.

That familiar feeling starts to simmer,
My bottom lip starts to quiver.

My eyes sting as the tears burst through,
I'm all alone not sitting here with you.

The evenings are my worst despair,
As I sit here alone in my chair.

I long to hold your hand just one more time,
To see your smile would be sublime.

I softly whisper as I talk to you,
Asking you questions about what I'm to do.

For a fleeting moment, I think I hear you speak,
A sound from upstairs as a floorboard squeaks

I look around thinking it's your face I'll see,
Then I realize there's no one here only me.

This night will pass and a new day will dawn,
I'm feeling tired and start to yawn.

It's time to rest my head and go to sleep,
I smile as I know in my dreams is where we'll meet.

New Year's Eve!

My heart is heavy as I shed a tear,
It's New Year's Eve and you're not here.

I started this year as your wife,
Now I'm alone and must learn to live this life.

All around me are happy and full of hope,
I'm filled with anticipation of will I cope.

What will the New Year bring for me?
The one thing I want cannot be.

I'd give anything to once again see your smile,
Just sit and chat with you for a while.

To hear your voice with encouraging words,
I still don't know how this has happened it's all absurd.

How can it be you're not here with me?
When all around it's you I see.

The time this year it's gone so fast,
It feels like you're slipping further into the past.

People struggle not knowing what to say,
The main thing I'm asked is am I ok?

I can't find the words to express all my fears
As I enter into this brand new year.

A fresh new start is what most will look forward to,
I long to go back in those strong arms with you!

Forward is the way I must keep stepping now,
One foot in front of the other, not quite knowing how.

Accepting a new life knowing you're still by my side
Your eternal love is my forever guide.

Into my heart, I'll look for courage and to be brave,
Remembering all the strength to me that you gave.

Happy New Year my darling angel up above,
I'm so grateful to have had and still feel your love

With brave wings...

She stands on the edge squeezing her eyes shut tight,
She knows if she leaps it will be a beautiful sight.

What if I can't do it? She starts to frown,
Her heart gently whispers build your wings on the way down.

With courage and faith, she throws her arms up wide,
Trusting her wings to open, and gracefully glide.

She feels the warmth of the sun and the wind in her hair,
As she takes the steps and falls through the air.

Her mind raced the chatter a familiar sound,
With thoughts of questioning what if I hit the ground.

She swoops and stumbles her heart skips a beat,
Her demons and fears she now must greet.

With a deep inner trust, she reaches for the sky,
And on these brave wings, she starts to fly.

5 Christmas Trees

Another year I put up the Christmas tree
Knowing you're not here to do it with me.

Another year of feeling the sharpness of an empty space,
As we set out the dinner table with 1 less place.

Another year of celebrations and Xmas presents,
Wishing we could all just see you here one more time to feel your presence.

Yet there's something about the Christmas tree with its twinkling lights,
That comforts me in the darkness of a cold lonely night.

I know there is nothing wrapped under the tree from you to me,
Because in my heart is where your gift will always be.

The gift of the eternal love you gave us all,
Cannot be found in a fancy box or glitter ball.

5 Christmas trees you've now not seen,
Yet each one I've known beside us is where you've always been.

Five years now decorating and pulling all the branches apart,
and with each one, I think of you and the memories we hold firmly in our hearts.

So as I decorate yet another Christmas tree,
I whisper with a smile "Happy Christmas my darling, fly free".

Heavenly Birthday

Another year has come to say a happy heavenly birthday to you,
I often think and say your name out loud you know this to be true.

If you were here I'd be pulling your leg at the addition of another year,
Instead, I hold a vision of you as I smile and shed a little tear.

I can't physically hug you and kiss your cheeky face,
I just feel your love and energy now in the space.

But feel you I surely do in everything all around,
Feeling your love gently embrace me as it eases my sorrowful frown.

I smile and remember you're always in my heart,
So with a cheeky grin, I whisper, happy birthday you old fart!

With love and laughter happy birthday Babes, we miss you Xx

Behind the smile

Behind the smile that most people see,
There are thoughts and emotions only known to me.

Hidden away in cold dark places,
They come and go with many different faces.

The words are hurtful painful and cruel,
As they try to take over with the aim of your life to rule.

You're so strong is often said to me,
Always happy and seeming full of glee.

The truth is we all have a voice in our heads,
That sometimes even tells us we're better off dead.

I'm lucky I know that's not the real Me,
And something I'd never choose to be.

Others aren't, believing the voice and what it has to say,
Harassing and tormenting them with every passing day.

Yes behind the smiles people hide many tales of woe,
Not knowing who to speak to and where to go.

Check-in on your loved ones and your friends,
They may not be as strong as they pretend.

A shoulder to lean on a hand to hold,
Is sometimes all they need to face the darkness and the cold.

Love is always the way out of life's darkest parts,
It shines a guiding light straight to the heart.

Valentines Day

It's Valentine's the day of love,
What if your loved one is up in heaven above?

What if you've not found that special one yet?
Does that mean this Valentine's day you must forget?

What if you've had the love and went through the heartbreak,
Does that mean, you must spend this day in sorrow, pain and with heartache?

What if you're happy to be single and alone?
Does this mean you can't join in with the celebrations at home?

Come closer and listen to these words from me to you,
Tune in with your heart not your mind and you'll know they are true.

Love is who you are and were born to be,
You don't need another to set you free.

The love you seek is inside of you,
It's what you are made of through and through.

Spend the day doing the things you love,
The heavens will rejoice and sing up above.

The magic will light up all around,
As the real love is you that now you have found.

Look deep within to the inner child whose been waiting for you,
Smile as you warmly say the words I'm here, you are safe and I love you

I'm just like you!

Just like you, I have thoughts that swirl around my head,
Sometimes joyful other times fuelled by fear and dread.

It's a negative voice we all have & know,
Its talk is full of doom & tales of woe.

It tricks you and deceives you into thinking,
There is no hope and your life is slowly sinking.

There is another way I promise you this,
A way that you can choose and feel joyful bliss.

It's the gentle quiet whispering of your heart,
Being still and listening carefully is the place to start.

Understand this is the Real You!
Its words are comforting and true.

It speaks in words of compassion and love,
Sometimes with guidance from up above.

Love is the way out of the darkness and fear,
It's the shining light that makes the pathway clear.

I promise you, I really am just like you,
I have all those thoughts and feelings too.

It's just I've learnt to not listen to this negative voice,
I've learnt, that I really do, have a choice.

I'll teach you as well if you allow me to,
I'll help show you how you can also choose.

Nobody taught me...

Nobody taught me in school that we have a voice inside our heads,
Constantly chattering filling me with dread.

Nobody taught me in school about the conscious and subconscious mind,
Showed me the differences of how conscious thought could give me more peace, no on my own, I had this discovery to find.

Nobody taught me in school about the nervous system - how knowing the benefits of the breath would take me back into my parasympathetic rest and digest and it could make all the difference.

Nobody taught me in school about the wounded inner child,
With all its untrue learnt belief systems that left it out in the cold running wild.

Nobody taught me in school that I had a choice,
Whether to listen or ignore the never-ending goading of the negative voice.

Nobody taught me in school that thoughts create feelings,
Instead, I just thought I was broken damaged and needed healing.

Nobody taught me in school the art of meditation,
How in adult life it could bring calm to my mind, keeping me off medication.

Why don't we teach all this in schools?
So our children learn as human beings they are in fact really cool.

Why don't we talk more about thoughts and that negative voice in our heads?
Instead of living a life in fear or even worse thinking, we're better off dead.

Why don't we teach our children about dependency and living from the heart?
Instead of being codependent forever fearing being apart.

Maybe if we started teaching all this in schools,
Then love would be the overwhelming majority that rules...

The reflection in the mirror

I see you looking wondering how all this came to be,
The tears flow and I wonder do you actually see me.

The hurt the pain the feelings of dread,
They rage like a tornado inside your head.

The loneliness the empty feeling inside your heart,
Fearing these thoughts and emotions as they tear you apart.

Then one day you look and at last, something shatters,
You finally start to see and understand what really matters.

The person you see staring back in the view,
Always knew you had everything inside of you.

You place your hand up over your beating heart,
And whispers gently it's ok I've got you, sweetheart.

I see you showing up daily with all that you face,
Trying so hard to heal with smile and grace.

You don't give up even when at times you desperately want to,
You know it's a journey and love will see you through.

The love you seek is not externally out there,
As you know you've been searching everywhere.

The love is right here gazing longingly at the view,
It's always been in the reflection that's staring back at you.

You are the only one with the power can't you see?
So give yourself the love coming from the reflection staring back at me.

So the next time you stand looking in the mirror wondering what to do,
Ask the question do you really see the wonder of the reflection staring back at you…

Pause for a moment of self-love

Stop for a moment and take a breath, become aware of the, inhale and exhale of air as it dances through your lungs.
Place your hand on your heart and connect as you feel the beat of it whispering to you with love.
Notice your skin with all its varying uniqueness, a road map detailing the history of your life, every mark, scar freckle a detail that can only be found in your story.
Find a mirror and look into your eyes and see all the wonderment of your soul staring back at you.
You, the unique beautiful wonderful limited edition nobody else can imitate version of YOU.

Show some love and compassion to yourself for all the battles you've won, all the times you felt you could no longer go on, yet here you are still standing.

Give thanks to the incredible warrior that is your body, quietly working away for you breathing life into you every day.
Beating the drum of your heartbeat that says to the world I'm here, I'm alive to receive this gift of another day.
Be proud of how incredible every cell that travels through you is, to interact with and support this incredible being that is you.

Yes, You, Your body is unique in every way just showing up quietly every day keeping you alive, giving your soul shelter for the time it inhabits this earth.

Show your body the love it so freely gives you...

In Closing

If you are here reading this page I thank you with all my heart and please know that I feel immense gratitude for you, as the fact you are holding this book in your hands means you have been a part of fulfilling my wish to get this book of poems birthed for publishing on the 5th anniversary of Shawn's Passing.

The time that has passed has certainly been a journey of self-discovery and I know that with every step, Shawn has been by my side guiding me along the way.

I made myself a promise that I would always aim to live my life in honour of Shawn, who lived for the children's happiness and mine. So to achieve the publishing of this book is another mark of respect to him in creating a happier sunshine moment to bring into the light, what could have been marked as a cloudy day as we reached this milestone of 5 years.

I cannot change the reality of what's happened; I can however choose to find the sunshine moments within it.

I've further pieces of writing sharing my thoughts and perspectives from our journey, which one day I will also release…

For now, keep seeking your sunshine moments, I promise you they are there to be found even if on some days you have to search a little harder.

Remember that the sun always shines, regardless of the clouds - You are the sunshine.

With Love

K xx

Acknowledgements

To my darling Shawn, Thank you for being you and the memories that will always be etched into my heart. You were and always will be my Knight in shining armour and yes you were right "It's all about the Love" It never left it's merely transcended.

To my amazing kids, Kiah & Bradley, I Did IT!!!
The book has been created and is a legacy for you to always hold onto as a reminder that when we set our minds to it we can achieve anything. The words you hold in your hands are a treasured memory to mark the power of love.
I am so immensely proud of you both, two incredible souls with resilience and such a depth of kindness that shines through for all who meet you, to be inspired.

I love you with all my heart to the moon and stars beyond xxx

Further acknowledgements:

With pride and love to my daughter, Kiah Ludbrook for the Sunshine Moment Artwork that is displayed on the front cover.
http://www.kiahludbrook.co.uk/

About Kerry

Kerry works as an Intuitive Reiki Master and wellness coach, following her passion to help others achieve a peaceful and joyful life using the wide variety of methods she has trained in along her self-healing journey.

She adores holding space for others to go within and explore their inner world with nothing but love, compassion and non-judgment. Her greatest pleasure is seeing the light come back on in another's eyes as they remember who they truly are. She loves helping you find your way back to a balanced state of peace and joy in a world that can at times feel a little overwhelming.

Stay Connected with Kerry

Facebook: https://www.facebook.com/bbeautifulyou/.

My sunshine moments today were…

My sunshine moments today were...

My sunshine moments today were…

My sunshine moments today were…

Printed in Great Britain
by Amazon